T0355978

ADDITIONAL PRAISE FOR
RETHINKING INVESTING

"The strategy that is most likely to lead to financial prosperity is surprisingly simple. This succinct book elegantly filters out the noise and focuses the read on what really matters."

—**James Choi,** Professor of Finance, Yale University

"Charles Ellis is an investment industry legend, as a practitioner, executive and academic for longer than most asset managers have been around. I can think of no one whose advice I would rather take when it comes to my own personal investments. *Rethinking Investing* is Charley at his most practical best."

—**Robin Wigglesworth,** author of *Trillions*

"If Charley Ellis is writing it, I am reading it! And you should too. Each new article and book bring a new perspective, a new insight and a new brilliant analogy! This book, is a gift from Charley to the millions of current and future investors who will find themselves better off."

—**Jenny Van Leeuwen Harrington,** Chief Executive Officer, Gilman Hill Asset Management

RETHINKING INVESTING

Books by Charles D. Ellis

Figuring It Out: Sixty Years of Answering Investors' Most Important Questions (Wiley, **2022**)

Inside Vanguard: Leadership Secrets From the Company That Continues to Rewrite the Rules of the Investing Business (McGraw-Hill, **2022**)

Winning the Loser's Game: Timeless Strategies for Successful Investing (McGraw-Hill, 8th Edition, **2021**)

The Elements of Investing: Easy Lessons for Every Investor, 10th Anniversary Edition (Wiley, **2021**)

The Index Revolution: Why Investors Should Join It Now (Wiley, **2016**)

Falling Short: The Coming Retirement Crisis and What to Do About It (Oxford University Press, **2014**)

The Elements of Investing: Easy Lessons for Every Investor (Wiley, **2013**)

What It Takes: Seven Secrets of Success from the World's Greatest Professional Firms (Wiley, **2013**)

The Partnership: The Making of Goldman Sachs (Penguin, **2008**)

Joe Wilson and the Creation of Xerox (Wiley, **2006**)

Capital: The Story of Long-Term Investment Excellence (Wiley, **2004**)

Wall Street People: True Stories of the Great Barons of Finance, Vol. 2 (Wiley, **2003**)

Wall Street People: True Stories of Today's Masters and Moguls, Vol. 1 (Wiley, **2001**)

Financial Services without Borders: How to Succeed in Professional Financial Services (Wiley, **2001**)

The Investor's Anthology; Original Ideas From the Industry's Greatest Minds (Wiley, **1997**)

Investment Policy: How to Win the Loser's Game (McGraw-Hill, **1992**)

Classics II: Another Investor's Anthology (Irwin Professional, **1991**)

Classics: An Investor's Anthology (Business One Irwin, **1988**)

The Second Crash: How the Stock Market Went the 1929 Route in 1970 (Simon and Schuster, **1973**)

Institutional Investing (Dow Jones-Irwin, **1971**)

Repurchase of Common Stock (Ronald Press, **1971**)

CHARLES D. ELLIS

RETHINKING INVESTING

A VERY SHORT GUIDE TO VERY LONG-TERM INVESTING

FOREWORD BY BURTON G. MALKIEL

WILEY

Published by John Wiley & Sons, Inc., Hoboken, New Jersey.
Published simultaneously in Canada.

For general information on our other products and services or for technical support, please contact our Customer Care Department within the United States at (800) 762-2974, outside the United States at (317) 572-3993 or fax (317) 572-4002.

Wiley also publishes its books in a variety of electronic formats. Some content that appears in print may not be available in electronic formats. For more information about Wiley products, visit our web site at www.wiley.com.

Library of Congress Cataloging-in-Publication Data is Available:

ISBN 9781394328291(Hardback)
ISBN 9781394328314(epdf)
ISBN 9781394328307(epub)

Cover Design: Wiley
Cover Image: © anilakkus/Getty Images

SKY10098699_022025

CONTENTS

CONTENTS

FOREWORD

How often have we heard people say, "If only I had known how small changes I could have made earlier in life could have made such profound changes in my financial security today in retirement." And "Wouldn't it be nice if I could have a short and simple primer from a knowledgeable expert that explained how almost unnoticeable changes in my lifestyle today will profoundly affect my long run financial well-being."

Charley Ellis, one of the legends in the investment profession, has come to the rescue. In these brief pages, you will learn all you need to know about investing wisely and setting yourself on the road to a secure financial future. Here you will learn not only what to do but also how to avoid the common errors that can ruin any financial plan. And all the important lessons are presented in an accessible, clear, and engrossing writing style. Reading this brief Charley Ellis chronicle of lessons learned from a lifetime of helping investors achieve their financial goals will be the most beneficial way anyone could spend a few hours of their time.

The average working household in the United States has no retirement assets apart from Social Security. The savings and related assets that do exist are closely correlated with income and wealth. This fact is prominently recognized by politicians who have favored imposing wealth taxes on the most affluent. However one views the fairness of the distribution of income and the tax system, there is another helpful way to lessen wealth inequality. Small changes early in life can absolutely ensure that even people with the most modest incomes can look forward to a seven-figure retirement portfolio.

On November 26, 2023, the *New York Times* published a charming story about Geoffrey Holt, who died leaving his entire estate of almost $4 million to his adopted hometown, Hinsdale, New Hampshire, to support community service organizations and programs. What shocked residents of the town was that Mr. Holt worked his whole life at a low salary, most recently as the caretaker for a mobile home park. His secret was that he had saved modest amounts of money regularly and invested his savings in the stock market.

The story of people with modest middle-class salaries amassing large fortunes is not an anomaly. In their book *The Millionaire Next Door*, Thomas J. Stanley and William Danko surveyed millionaire households in the United States and made the surprising conclusion that the typical millionaire isn't living extravagantly with fancy homes and cars, all thanks to an inherited trust fund. Most millionaires are first-generation rich. They often started their own business. Wealth in America is more often the result of a strong work ethic, frugal spending habits, and regular savings and investing. The millionaires next door have no interest in conspicuous consumption. They spend modestly and save regularly, and they appear to be far happier than their more ostentatious peers. This is the same template of a successful financial life that you will find in the pages of this book.

But is this really possible for individuals with no financial expertise who are unwilling to make an entire lifestyle change? Absolutely. Suppose a person substitutes breakfast at home for a once-a-week visit to the local coffee shop for a latte and sausage roll, saving about $23 a week ($100 a month). If those monthly savings had been invested in a tax-advantaged retirement plan holding a Vanguard 500 index fund starting in 1978 (when the first index fund became available), that person would have had over $1.5 million at the end of 2023. Had the savings been matched by an employer, the final sum would be over $3 million. Paraphrasing the financial coach Suze Orman, spending $7 on a latte two days a week is like peeing over a million dollars down the drain. In these pages you will be reminded of the awesome power of compounding and how even modest savings can grow into a seemingly unattainable fortune.

Charley Ellis will show you here how you don't need expertise to choose the best stocks. That expertise does not exist. All you need to do is to invest in low-cost broad-based index funds (or buy an exchange-traded index fund—ETF—from a discount broker). This strategy will not produce mediocre results. On the contrary, you are likely to earn well-above-average returns. Over the 20 years ending in mid-2023, investing in a broad-based U.S. (total market) equity fund produced net returns better than over 90% of professionally managed stock funds that promise to beat the market. And the average annual return was 1.8 percentage points better than the return of the average actively managed fund, according to a recent study by Standard & Poor's.

In this small gem of a book you will learn how to minimize costs and taxes. You will be exposed to all the common errors (such as trying to time the market or actively moving in and out of investment funds) and all the other behavioral biases that lead people astray. A recent study by Morningstar reveals that over the past decade, investors in actively managed mutual funds and ETFs lost about 17% of the gains they could have achieved because they timed their purchases and sales poorly.

Charley also offers extremely valuable advice about the best way to determine how much you will be able to spend out of your nest egg in retirement. An optimal withdrawal strategy can ensure that the resources available to you for spending can remain stable and minimize the risk that you will run out of money even if you live to 100. Advice on integrating Social Security benefits into your financial plan and maximizing the benefits you will receive is easily accessible to readers with no financial experience.

This book is short on pages but long on actionable spending, saving, and investment advice. You will be grateful to have read it for years to come.

—Burton G. Malkiel

Author of A Random Walk Down Wall Street
50th Anniversary Edition (2023)

INTRODUCTION

For over 60 years, I have had the good fortune to work with leading investors around the world, advising institutions, family foundations, and governments about their investment policies and practices. For many years, while serving as chair of the Yale University Investment Committee, I witnessed the prowess of David Swensen, one of the world's most successful investment leaders. Teaching advanced investment courses at Harvard and Yale was also a great pleasure. However, my greatest delight has been helping individuals make wiser investment decisions for themselves and their families.

An early proponent of index funds, I have become increasingly convinced of the wisdom of relying on them for the powerful reasons that are highlighted in this book. In recent years, I have identified a constellation of nine investment-related issues that, taken together, can dramatically increase your investment success:

1. Recognizing the remarkable "snowballing" power of compounding over time—particularly when investing in equities over a longer period

2. The importance of saving—as much as possible as early as possible

3. Understanding the dramatic changes in the structure of the stock market (including the rise to dominance by professional investors) and how they make it very difficult for active managers to beat the market over time

4. Using broad-based index funds and exchange-traded funds as the principal investment choice— with their low fees, low operating costs, low taxes, *and* superior performance over time

5. Avoiding the many pitfalls identified by behavioral economists that so regularly cause serious harm to investors' results and diminish significantly the average individual investor's return

6. Minimizing costs, fees, and taxes. Since it's so very hard to beat the market, savvy investors will focus on minimizing costs incurred by most other investors.

7. Recognizing that your Total Financial Portfolio—which includes the present value of your future Social Security payments and the equity value of your house—already provides large "bond equivalents" so you need fewer (and maybe no) bond holdings

8. Adopting a sensible Spending Rule to smooth year-to-year payouts from your investments, which may reduce (or may eliminate) the traditional "stabilizing" role of bonds

9. Deferring when you start receiving Social Security benefits—and considering working longer

While each of these components can be adopted independently, the real Eureka! payoff comes by using them together and persistently. This short book gives a clear explanation of each. I hope you find it a helpful roadmap for your long-term investing success.

—Charley Ellis

CHAPTER ONE

COMPOUNDING AND TIME = YOUR GREAT POWER CURVE OPPORTUNITY

"The power of compounding is unmatched by any factor in the production of wealth through investment," says Warren Buffett. "Compounding over a long investment program is your best strategy—bar none." And America's favorite investor has certainly proven the validity of his belief.

The extraordinary power of compounding is the amazing ability to make money with money. Compounding has two dimensions: the rate of return you receive on your investment and the time you have to invest. The higher the *rate* of return, the more you will eventually have. The longer the *time* your investment compounds, the more you will eventually have. Or, to clarify by putting it the other way around, the lower the rate and the shorter the time, the *less* you will have.

Eventually your initial investment will double. It's in the math—and the math of compounding, importantly, saves the best for last: 1...2...4...8...16...32. Note that the last redoubling, of course, provides fully half of the total compounding over the whole period. That's why it matters to get the compounding process started as soon as possible and stay with it as long as possible. So, $1 is not just $1: $1 is a potential $32—or even more *if* you start early enough.[1] The large risk is that readers might focus on the small benefits that come with the first and second

---

[1] The ugly opposite of saving is credit card debt. With the interest rates as high as 22%, $1,000 in debt doubles in less than 3½ years and redoubles to $4,000 in 3½ more years and $8,000 in 3½ more. So never get started.

doublings and not get started soon enough to enjoy the subsequent doublings from 8 to 16 or even from 16 to 32. This phenomenon is proof-positive of the most important reason to save early—saving as much as you can comfortably save in as many ways as you can—because all those savings will join together in compounding your future wealth and future payouts from your investments.

As is shown in the next chapter, it's terribly hard to obtain higher than market returns, but it is well within your power to save more or save sooner—or both—so you can get the great power of compounding working for you.

Are you familiar with the Rule of 72? We all should be. The Rule of 72 is a simple way to figure out how long it will take to double your money at a specific rate of return. If your money is earning 3%, dividing 72 by 3 (your rate of return) shows it will take 24 years to double your money. Or if you earn 7%, dividing 72 by 7% shows that your money will double in 10.3 years. If the rate of gain is 8%, $1 will double in 9 years. ($100 will double in 9 years; $10,000 will double in that same time; $1 million will double in 9 years *and* then double again in another 9 years.) If the rate of gain is 10%, doubling takes only

7.2 years. And the same for redoubling and then doubling again—and again. Each doubling, of course, results in twice as much money as the previous one. The remarkable Warren Buffett, in addition to astute investment decisions, made more time for compounding by starting to invest in his early teens—and continuing well into his 90s, adding many years to his time for compounding.

We should all remember the fable of the emperor and his wise man. The wise man solved a major problem that had long puzzled the emperor. In gratitude, the emperor declared that he would provide any reward the wise man wished. The wise man said he had only done his duty and was too humble to accept a reward. The emperor insisted. So, reluctantly, the wise man agreed to accept one grain of wheat. The emperor said that was *way* too little. So, the humble wise man then agreed to make a small change: one grain of wheat that would be doubled and doubled again on each square of the chess board—eight squares wide and eight squares deep for a total of 64 doublings.

The emperor quickly agreed, made a public announcement of his commitment, and invited all the nobles of the realm to come and witness the payment of the wise man's reward.

The grains of wheat were few at first, but they doubled and doubled again and redoubled to a cup of wheat and then to a sack of wheat and on to a wagonload and then to a full silo of wheat, to multiple silos, and on and on to more wheat than the entire realm produced each year. And still there were squares yet to be counted.

The emperor could see the inevitable outcome. Being a man of honor and knowing that all the nobles knew what he had promised, he turned to the humble wise man and said, "The whole realm is all yours!"

Your investing Power Curve is the result of achieving the compounding returns of your investments over time. But, first, you have to save what you can to ride up your Power Curve and reap the benefits of compounding.

Compounding is also why it pays to emphasize equities, as we review in Chapter 7. Why? The long-term returns on equities are significantly higher *and* thus the rate of compounding is greater—so your money will double sooner and push your Power Curve up more rapidly. Additionally, as we see in Chapter 5, you can move up to a higher Power Curve by reducing costs, fees, and taxes by using index funds.

Look at the curves in Exhibit 1.1. You'll quickly see the remarkably positive impact on compounding due to higher rates of return and a longer period of investing. More costs, more fees, or more taxes will lower your Power Curves *and* result in a much lower eventual value for you as the investor. That's why starting earlier is so important *and* why avoiding unnecessary costs is so important.

Exhibit 1.1: The Power Curve: See the Value of $100,000 Based on Time and Rate of Return

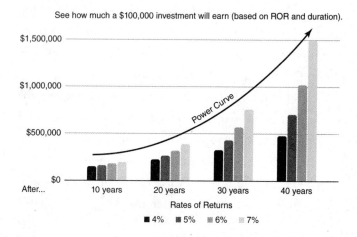

See how much a $100,000 investment will earn (based on ROR and duration).

Power Curves are every investor's great friend, and understanding Power Curves increases your incentive to save. Since fully half of all the total dollars at the end comes in the last round of doubling, the only way to get more of that important final doubling is to start your Power Curve sooner.

Even if you are too advanced in age to reap all the benefits yourself, you can still tell your children and grandchildren how to ride the Power Curve up, up, and away.

CHAPTER TWO

SAVING: YOUR FIRST PRIORITY

S aving, like so many things in life, is a matter of choice—*your* choice—as is the self-discipline to keep saving. This chapter shows many different ways to save so you can decide which ways of saving will work best for your life.

Exhibit 2.1 shows the impact over time of different rates of return if you make an initial investment of $1,000 at an early age. Which of these columns of lifetime investment results would you choose for yourself?

Exhibit 2.1: The Gift of Time: The Benefit of Investing Early

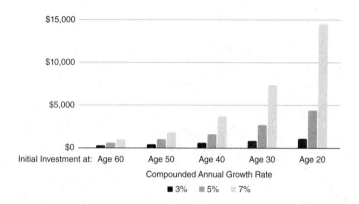

See how much a $1,000 investment will earn (based on ROI and age when the investment was made).

Exhibit 2.1 shows starkly that *time* is the investor's great gift—*if* investors use it. Strive to take full advantage of the time available to be a successful longer-term investor by saving and investing as much as you can as soon as you can and for as long as you can.

How you decide to think about saving is important. Some folks think of saving as a form of self-denial: enjoyment forgone, pleasures denied, and various forms of can't, don't, and won't. This negative orientation prevents them from seeing the important *positive* side of saving: how it will enable you and your family to enjoy more of the things you most care about and how it increases your opportunities to have more of your first choices throughout your life. Saving can also be seen as swapping things you don't particularly need now for things you and those you love will most enjoy in the future. By combining good saving habits and good investing practices, you can have many more first choices in the years ahead.

As shown in Chapter 1, the later years on your Power Curve produce the largest gains, thanks to the almost magical realities of compounding. So, when you save $1 or $100 or $1,000, always think of the value to you of this saving *after* they have zoomed up the Power Curve over all the years between now and when they will be spent.

The most important saving and investing decision most of us ever make is made when we decide where to work—and whether the prospective employer offers a 401(k) retirement plan and, if so, how that plan works. While many companies have a 401(k) plan, others—particularly smaller firms—may not. Moreover, the terms of 401(k) plans differ a lot from one company to another. A 401(k) plan is a key benefit, because those savings compound tax-free until you access the funds later in life. If your employer offers a 401(k) retirement plan, be sure to take full advantage of any match offered.[1] It is like found money and should be a powerful incentive to save.

Here are the important questions about prospective employers you'll want answered:

- Does the company have a 401(k) plan?
- How much does the company contribute, and what match does it offer you? The average match has the employer contributing about 5% of your pay to your retirement plan, but some plan sponsors match up to 10%, and some do not match at all. Over the many years of your career, particularly because of compounding, the difference in matching really matters to you.

---

[1] For example, an employer's 401(k) plan may say that if the employee contributes 4% of his or her salary to the retirement plan, the employer will match that amount and contribute it to the retirement account.

- How soon does the employer's contribution vest and become yours? Many vest immediately, but some take as long as six years to vest, which would prove problematic if you change jobs before vesting.
- What options are offered in the plan for how you can invest your 401(k) funds? Importantly, are low-cost index funds an option?

Your own saving can come in many forms, so you have many choices. Ponder your choices and adopt the ones that will work best for you. Here are some examples to consider:

- Match the match of your 401(k) plan. Of course!
- Consider having more money automatically deducted from your paycheck before you ever see it—as a voluntary additional contribution to your 401(k) account or to a personal savings account.
- Invest in low-cost index funds and exchange-traded funds (ETFs) rather than much more costly actively managed funds—as we explore in Chapter 4. It's not just what you'll save each year, it's what you'll save

over many years from indexing—and all those annual savings get compounded for many years.

- Avoid credit card debt—like the plague. The interest rates charged can be as high as 22%—way too high for you, or anyone else, to *ever* accept. So, don't!
- If your spouse and you are both employed, consider saving part of the lower income and investing it.
- Limit your spending to the income you earned two or three (or even more) years ago. Save and invest the rest.
- If you earn a bonus, invest it.
- Buy preowned cars. (New cars notoriously lose a big chunk of value as they are driven off the dealer's lot.)
- Consider a smaller house that meets your family's needs or defer a few years longer when trading up to a larger house—and, in the meantime, invest the saving.
- Self-insure auto damages under $10,000—or whatever you can comfortably afford to pay in the unlikely event of a major accident. (The cost of insuring smaller amounts of damage is very high,

because the cost of processing claims is nearly as large for small claims as for larger ones.)

- If life insurance makes sense when you have a young family, consider term life insurance, particularly the low-cost term insurance available through savings banks and credit unions.
- Consider less expensive hobbies and vacations. Compare the lifetime costs of golfing or skiing with biking or hiking and camping in our beautiful national parks.
- When shopping, buy only what you and your spouse or partner have on your shopping list or what you both agree offers good value. Look for bargains. And take quiet pride in your ability to walk right past unnecessary luxuries. Lots of small-expense items can add up and cut into your potential savings.

Of the many ways to save, select the ways that are best for you. Develop good saving habits and learn to enjoy them by making saving a positive feedback experience. Whatever pathways to saving you decide are best for you and your family, be sure to track your achievements regularly, compared to your own plan—and celebrate your success, knowing you'll enjoy more first choices in the future as you save more now. Each of us can increase our wealth in three ways: by saving more, by investing wisely, or by a double-barreled combination of *both*.

CHAPTER THREE

CHANGE, CHANGE, AND MORE CHANGE

While investors' attention is usually focused on the daily changes in stock prices and media stories about which investment managers are performing well or poorly, the far more important and enduring changes have been in the inner workings of the stock market as a market. Over the past half century, the stock market has gone through several major structural changes that every investor needs to understand. The changes include the growing market dominance of expert professional investment managers who have significantly improved price discovery and also the impact of more federal regulation and technological advances. Each of those changes has made the market harder and harder to beat—especially after taking into account costs, fees, and taxes.

Over time, there has been enormous change in the mix of trading by individuals versus institutional investors, and the impact of this great change has been profound. Half a century ago, the trading volume on the New York Stock Exchange (NYSE) had gradually increased to three million shares a day (so Saturday trading, once needed by Wall Street brokerage firms to achieve a break-even weekly trading volume, had been discontinued.) Today, the volume of trading in NYSE-listed shares has increased to nearly 1 *billion* shares a day—up over 300 *times* in volume. (Comparable increases have occurred in many of the major exchanges around the world.)

Far more important than the surge in the volume of trading or the substantial integration across markets has been the profound change *within* the major markets—starting with market participants. Fifty years ago, about 90%

of trading on the NYSE was by individual amateur investors while institutions did the rest. Of that 10% done by institutions, almost all was done by regional bank trust departments. At that time, the United States had over 14,000 banks, and banks were not allowed to serve consumers in more than one state. Most banks were, by current standards, small, and few were sophisticated. Many had small trust departments to serve their local communities with personal trusts. The banks were understandably conservative; they were "buy and hold" managers of blue-chip stocks that paid good dividends and avoided unnecessary capital gains taxes by holding those stocks for many years. In addition, they usually combined those long-term stock holdings with "laddered maturity" bond portfolios—maturities spaced over time. Trust departments were *not* aggressive trading competitors in the stock or bond markets. The next largest group of institutional investors were insurance companies, which also bought and held for the long, long term. They were *not* aggressive competitors either.

The kinds of people and the kind of work done in these institutions differed profoundly from today's highly skilled and highly competitive investment professionals. If you were one of the few truly talented investment managers many years ago, it was almost easy to beat the pack.

While, as mentioned, 90% of trading half a century ago was done by individual amateurs, now more than 90% of trading is done by professional institutional investors, particularly hedge fund managers using research from dedicated experts. The shift in market participation from easy-to-beat, part-time amateurs with little or no investment information to hard-to-beat, sophisticated, and expert professional investors has been among the most important changes over the past half century.

Those doing 90% of the trading today are full-time, highly trained professionals. Each institution has all sorts of highly motivated and professional experts who are intensely competitive and have instantaneous access to information. While most individual investors usually make decisions to buy or sell for *outside*-the-market reasons—such as investing a bonus or selling so a tuition bill can be paid—professional investors are always comparison shopping and making *inside*-the-market decisions. Some individual investors are better informed than most,[1] but they are not nearly as well-informed as the institutional professionals who now dominate the stock market and are the competition for any individual investor.

Inside-the-market changes have been numerous, remarkably forceful, and little appreciated by outsiders. They have combined into a powerful mechanism that has revolutionized the securities markets of the world. Anyone who has not been involved as a market insider would be amazed by the aggregate change and what all this means for today's investors. Gone also are the days when each country's national market was on its own. Today, investors from every nation can invest in most stock markets around the world. So, every market is interconnected with the other markets in what is increasingly one global stock market. Add to this the remarkable ways the stock and bond markets are now interconnected with the real estate market and the international oil market and the financial

---

[1] The largest firm serving the retail market 50 years ago was Merrill Lynch. It produced *no* research at any time. Even Goldman Sachs—a leader in the institutional market—produced only a four-page document, put together by one salesman in an effort to help his clients.

21

futures market and all the rest of the huge derivatives market. All this change is wrapped into the enormous global foreign exchange market. The interconnections are many, and they continue to get closer and stronger.

Over the past 60 or so years, the professional investment managers[2] have, as a group, made the pricing of individual securities across the markets of the world more and more accurate relative to risk and to alternative securities. Therefore, it is increasingly difficult for an active investment manager to "beat" or improve on the expert consensus on stock prices.

This fact, of course, is right in line with what all markets are supposed to do. As more professional buyers and more sellers—with more and better information and better technology and more "fair trading" regulations—do more transactions with more skill as they compete with each other, the market they operate in gets better and better at the central purpose of every market: accurate price

---

[2] Professional investment managers are regularly called "active managers" because they are actively involved in buying and selling stocks and in other investing of their portfolios. They will be referred to as such throughout this book.

discovery. As the stock and bond markets keep increasing their pricing accuracy, or "efficiency," there are fewer and smaller opportunities for active managers to identify overpriced stocks to sell or underpriced stocks to buy skillfully enough to cover all their fees and costs of operation. As price discovery gets better and better, participants are less able to beat the market—and much, much less able to do so repeatedly, particularly after subtracting their costs and fees. (The same improvements in price discovery have also changed the bond market.)

Major changes have combined to transform the world's stock markets from an attractive, opportunity-rich environment for capable active investment managers into an exceedingly difficult environment for any active manager seeking ways to do better. As we see in Chapter 5, the costs and fees for active investment management now present a daunting hurdle for these managers to overcome, particularly in a highly competitive, moderate rate-of-return market such as is projected for the future.

Two additional factors have fueled the improvements in accurate price discovery and market efficiency: federal regulation and technology.

In regulation, the main change has been Reg FD—short for Regulation on Fair Disclosure. This is the Securities and Exchange Commission regulation, promulgated in 2000, that requires all publicly-owned companies to make systematic and effective efforts to ensure that *any* useful investment information made available to *any* investor is deliberately made available to *all* investors simultaneously.

This regulation certainly makes sense to ensure the market is fair. But it is a major shift from the practices of the past that had given active managers a major advantage: They could legally have private meetings with senior corporate executives to probe deeply into corporate strategy, possible acquisitions, capital expenditures, and product pricing, among other things. And corporate executives would give candid, informative answers. The intention of the corporate executives was to ensure accurate, or "fair," pricing of their company's shares—a potentially valuable corporate asset. At the same time, these private discussions gave the active manager a significant "unfair" information advantage that could easily be translated into superior investment performance by buying ahead of good news and selling ahead of bad news.

Before Reg FD, active investment managers were dependent on this advantage. Now it's *illegal* to hold such meetings. Instead of private meetings, companies must make sure that all the information they provide goes out simultaneously to all investors—usually by having a quarterly conference call open to all investors—and not provide any information unavailable to all. Of course, this means that active investors are no longer able to get an important, competitive information advantage by developing special relationships with company executives.

Another major change over the past half century has come in the voluminous amount of research available to institutional investors who have extraordinary access to expert analysts all over the globe. These expert analysts monitor and evaluate every major company in every major economy and market around the world. They compete intensively with each other for the big business of institutional investors by seeking out new information and funneling that information *and* their interpretation of its significance to all their institutional investor clients. (In addition, many smaller firms have specialized groups of analysts working in specific areas, such as healthcare or technology.)

Technology also has clearly been a driving force for change in investment management. The Internet enables hundreds of people in each major organization to gather relevant information instantaneously from around the world and share that information across the Internet's network of experts within their own organization—and get immediate responses. Years ago, active managers were proud of their skills with slide rulers. Computers were used only for accounting and back-office functions. A major change in the market has been the extraordinary increase in computing power that every institutional investor has and uses all the time.

Computer models are now capable of organizing and screening huge amounts of data in useful ways for analysts to make projections of future probabilities. For example, satellites provide up-to-the-minute data on oil tanker movements and the number of cars in shopping mall parking lots. Artificial intelligence is increasingly used and will inevitably grow in use by institutional investors.

While individual investment managers may be thrilled by the novelty and the power of their own firm's technology, the larger reality is that almost all competitors already have or will soon get equal technology. Rather than providing a competitive *advantage*, technology is over and over again a great *equalizer*. Every institutional investor has the same wonderful technology and the same instantaneous access to superb information. So, they all face one daunting challenge: Almost all the other institutional investors know almost everything at almost the same time.

The result of all these major changes is that few, if any, professional investors can develop, let alone sustain, a significant competitive advantage in information or in information processing. This increasing equalization makes it more than difficult for any major manager to get ahead of the superb and persistently improving competition. As we've seen, professional managers are nearly equal in technology and in information—and are doomed to become more and more equal in the days ahead.

Meanwhile, competition among institutional investors has produced a Darwinian process of sorting out, so only the most capable and successful institutional investors have survived. This, of course, means that the average skill of the average institutional investor has been rising to higher and higher levels. Excellence is matched by excellence—and so, ironically, gets canceled out.

For those who seek a highly capable investment manager with superb computer technology, excellent access to expert research, highly motivated analysts, and portfolio managers, the good news is that they are easy to find—because there are so many of them. The problem is, of course, that finding a highly capable manager is not enough. The investor needs to find a significantly *more* capable investment manager—more capable than others by enough to make a significant positive difference after subtracting the manager's costs and fees. Doing this is hard because everybody is so nearly equal to everyone else in research information, in computing power, and in striving to succeed. Finally, ironically but understandably, the best managers are often not accepting new clients.

There you have it: The whole world around active investing has changed in many major ways, and all those changes compound to make it more and more difficult for any of those high-talent, hard-working active managers to outperform the market that they have collectively made so hard to keep up with—let alone beat.

Price discovery is, of course, the main function of any market for oil or houses or wine or currencies or diamonds or anything else. Price discovery does not mean determining the perfect price or even what will be seen in retrospect as the "correct" price. Rather, today's market price is the price that makes it unlikely that anyone will be able to make reliably superior pricing decisions—given all the information available—and particularly unlikely that anyone would be able to do so on a regular basis by enough to cover all the fees *and* the costs of operations— particularly in a moderate-return market.

Sure, this difficult feat has been done by some managers and will be done in some years by many managers— but not by many managers over many years and almost certainly not by the same managers. Experts in the field of evaluating active investment managers have been unable to identify in advance which managers would outperform in the future. That's why the SPIVA data—the data from Standard & Poor's Dow Jones Indices about manager performance—is so important. Of all the actively managed mutual funds in operation over the past 20 years, what percentage of them did at least slightly better than the market (or market segment) they chose to beat? The grim reality is that less than 15% of any group of managers—after fees and costs but before taxes—performed at least as well as their chosen part of the market. (SPIVA reported on February 23, 2023, that 89% of U.S. mutual funds had *underperformed* the S&P 500 index over the previous 20 years.) Over shorter time periods, the failures are clearly daunting: over 10 years, 90%, and over 5 years, 85%. Note: This does *not* mean that active managers are getting better—only that luck has more chance of making an impact in shorter time periods.

Even worse, those active managers who underperformed often fell short by *multiples* of the amount of superiority achieved by the "winners"—usually, in the worst cases, by taking more risks in desperate hope of a miraculous recovery. Finally, experienced statisticians would expect that the past group of "winners" would suffer the same harsh casualty rate in the future with about 85–90% of the past 20 years' winners joining the losers in the future.

Careful study will lead any objective observer to the obvious conclusion: Given the transformation in the world of active investing, it makes sense that only a small minority of active managers—who, importantly, cannot be identified in advance—will, with luck, achieve favorable results after fees and costs of operations. The average client experience with active managers, over time, has been and will be negative, relative to investing in a broad-based, low-cost index fund.

Why then do so many investors still entrust their investments to active management? One response is that we hear or read reports about those few managers who happen to have had good results recently, so our information is seriously biased. Another is that we, being human, tend to believe we can or should be able to select winners, as we review in Chapter 6. Finally, "hope springs eternal."

CHAPTER FOUR

YOUR GREAT GIFTS: INDEX FUNDS AND ETFs

We now know that it is harder and harder for active management to achieve superior investment results over time, and as is explained in Chapter 6, most of us are not prepared as individuals to make good investment decisions. So, what should we do? As the prospects for active managers to beat the market regularly have declined, an entirely new approach to investing developed, was battle-tested, and proven effective: low-cost index funds.

Index funds—and later exchange-traded funds (ETFs)[1]—take a different approach. Index funds and ETFs do not struggle to do "better" than the market. They simply match the market, *and* they charge much lower fees *and* minimize operating costs. Index funds also enable the investor to avoid the costly behavioral economics mistakes detailed in Chapter 6.

An index fund is simply a portfolio of stocks (or bonds) designed to replicate the composition of a particular financial market index (such as the S&P 500). For example, assume you have $1,000 to invest. You could put all of it into purchasing a handful of stocks and then confront the market behavior of those companies' market prices. Or you could put your money into the 500 Index Fund where you would be buying a slice of each of the 500 stocks in that index fund, proportionate

---

[1] An exchange-traded fund is traded on a major exchange continuously during the day, while an index fund is repriced twice each trading day. A broad-based ETF operates just like an index fund. But some ETFs are limited to an industry group or are actively managed portfolios—and they have the downside risks of an actively managed portfolio.

to the stock market's weighting among the 500 largest listed companies.

There are many different index funds[2] designed to replicate either all or a major part of the overall market. You can buy index funds that reflect the total U.S. stock market or the S&P 500, or you can choose index funds that focus on growth or value stocks, large- or small-capitalization stocks, or the stocks of any major industry or country or any region of the world. You get the important value of more diversification by going with a total market domestic or a total market global index fund—and should avoid narrowly focused index funds or ETFs. Management fees for broad-based index funds are much lower: They can be as low as 0.05% (or even lower) versus fees sometimes as high as 1.0% charged by active managers. The portfolio turnover of index funds is very low relative to most actively managed fund so the annual taxes on gains are also comparatively very low.

Also, index funds and ETFs—much like dishwashers and indoor plumbing—make life easier and free up time

---

[2] There are more stock indices than listed stocks.

for far more valuable activities, such as concentrating on long-term financial planning and investment policy.

One major advantage of index funds is that they are *not* interesting. Just as nobody wants to experience an "interesting" flight on an airplane, the lack of daily excitement in indexing substantially reduces the temptation to "do something" and act in ways that can be detrimental to your portfolio (as we review in Chapter 6). Over time, benign neglect by index investors—just buy a broad index fund and hold it—has been splendidly rewarding.

Where did index funds come from? Back in the 1960s, Bell System engineers were put in charge of the companies' pension funds as part of their managerial rotations. They examined the data on investment results and, because the several large pension funds of the Bell System operating companies each had numerous active managers, they collectively had all sorts of data on investment results. They found that active managers were not, as a group, beating the market; in fact, collectively, they were repeatedly falling *behind* the market. Being experienced with objective, data-based decision-making, the engineers naturally became early adopters of indexing—and it worked well!

With indexing, investment results repetitively and consistently matched clients' objectives *and* fees, and costs were much lower. As a result, index funds' performance was superior. So, the Bell System operating companies increased their use of index funds and told other companies about their favorable experiences. Gradually—ever so gradually—other pension funds began to switch over to indexing.

There is a familiar process by which innovations get accepted.[3] While the *rate* of progress varies considerably—doctors adopted penicillin quite rapidly while farmers adopted hybrid seed corn quite slowly—the *process* repeatedly follows a known pattern. Early adopters, or innovators, get a personal kick out of being first and are always looking for chances to experiment with the new. They experience lots of failures but don't really mind because they want to be pioneers and the first in their neighborhood to have what's new. Next come the influencers, who watch the innovators and adopt only those new things that actually work. They're called influencers

---

[3] The process was enunciated by Thomas Kuhn in his classic book *The Structure of Scientific Revolutions*, first published in 1962.

because when they adopt something new, it has already been proven to work well, so lots of others will confidently follow them and adopt the new thing. And that's the way it has been with index funds.

Still, you might ask, why has the process of widespread adoption of indexing taken so long and been so very gradual? One reason may be semantic. Index investing used to be called "passive" investing, in contrast to "active" investing by managers who were choosing individual stocks and other assets. We all want to be recognized as active. Nobody wants to be known as passive. Can you imagine how you would feel if your boss introduced you as "my passive deputy?" Or "my favorite candidate for president gets my vote because he's passive." So, one reason indexing has been accepted so slowly may be that it initially got stuck with the pejorative term "passive investing" rather than simply being called "index investing."

How did this semantic problem happen? Simple coincidence. Index funds were originally developed by engineers. Electrical engineers use the term "passive" all the time to describe the wall socket into which an "active" two- or three-pronged plug attached to a cord is pushed to make an electric connection. Engineers saw no adverse connotation: For them, "passive" and "active" were just descriptive.

But, for nonengineers—particularly highly competitive people or people looking for winners, passive is for losers—and certainly no way to succeed in a field as competitive as investment management where the typical goal is to be in the top quartile of investment results.

Aside from the semantic baggage, most investors have found it hard to believe that talented active managers with superb information won't beat the market since they see persistent winners in other lines of business, sports, and entertainment. Also, for active managers who were attracted to this exciting career and a chance to earn high fees and incomes, indexing was contrary to what they did and how they defined themselves. Low-fee indexing presented a direct existential threat to active investors' business profits and their sense of self-worth. So, active managers fought against indexing as though they and their careers were seriously threatened—as they surely were and certainly are!

The media were also culprits in the long delay to get indexing the respect and following it was due. Knowing that indexing's persistent successes would *not* make for compelling or even moderately interesting copy, the financial press kept heralding the "news" of so-and-so active manager doing well this year, knowing that they would likely report on a different manager doing well the following year.

The grim reality is clear: Active investing is not able to keep up with, let alone outperform, the market index. Among actively managed mutual funds, Morningstar reports that over the long term, most funds—by far—underperform their chosen benchmarks. Specifically, over the past 15 years, less than 10% of large-cap funds have kept up with their benchmark indexes: 3.5% of large-cap growth funds, 7.3% of large-cap value funds, and 8.9% of large-cap blend funds. (Note that since 20-year performance records are more favorable, the funds' performance is actually getting worse.)

In the next charts from Morningstar, the grim reality is that even after removing the 40% of mutual funds that were merged or liquidated (usually because of their poor

performance), substantial numbers of continuing funds—
both large blended funds and large growth funds—have
had poor performance records.

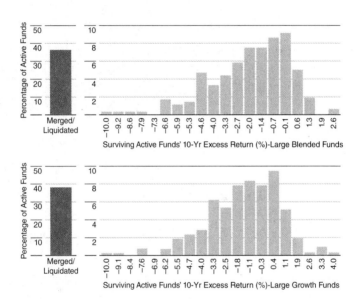

Surviving Active Funds' 10-Yr Excess Return (%)-Large Blended Funds

Surviving Active Funds' 10-Yr Excess Return (%)-Large Growth Funds

DALBAR reports comparably dour results for actively
managed equity mutual funds versus the S&P 500 Index
over 30 and 20 years.

	Average fund	S&P 500 index	Difference
30 years	8.0%	10.2%	2.2%
20 years	8.7%	9.7%	1.0%

Again, the trend is as expected, given the structural changes in the market and the skill of the increasingly dominant professionals.

While most investment thought leaders have accepted indexing as a superior way to invest, recently a few commentators have raised concerns about indexing. One was a warning that index funds—being always fully invested—are captives of the market and only active managers can get you out before the market collapses. But experience does not confirm this warning. When some active managers were out of the market, others were all in. As a result, the total amount of clients' money out of the market has been, year after year, about the same.

Of all the concerns about indexing, one that has the most surface plausibility is that as more and more investors entrust their assets to indexing, surely there must come a time—so-called "peak passive"[4]—when indexing will become so dominant that active management will somehow have a renaissance and again be successful. Then, the question usually becomes what percentage of investors' *assets* being indexed will it take for active investing to have a comeback? The informed response is that since index funds have so little turnover, their share of stock market trading is much smaller than their share of investors' assets. So, the share of assets indexed could be as high as 80%—or even higher—before flows into indexing could even slightly affect the market pricing of individual stocks.

Moreover, such analysis puts the focus on the wrong factor. The key question is: When will the price determination by active management become sufficiently

---

[4] On January 26, 2023, John Authers, in a Bloomberg Opinion piece entitled "Peak Passive, Here We Come," noted a paper by Daniel Taylor arguing that peak passive is near. (That paper was based on a 2009 article by Cremers and Petajisto that introduced the concept of "active share"—the portion of an actively managed fund that differs from its benchmark.) Taylor based his view on the theory that the flow of funds from active managers to index funds has created a tailwind favoring index funds and a headwind retarding actively managed funds and that the rate of change must, inevitably, slow down. While surely true in theory, the daily magnitude of money flowing into index funds and away from active managers as a percentage of market activity is way too small to make a salient difference.

imperfect or inefficient that some active managers can, once again, find ample ways to do significantly better? That would depend on the unlikely event that lots of active managers and research analysts would be fired or drop out or change to new careers in their 40s and 50s—leaving the field more open for a few winners. So far, however, more people are joining the ranks of active managers than are retiring, and many investment managers continue their careers for many years after normal retirement age.

One observer suggests that if major index fund managers were to collude, they could vote together against sensible business decisions. In theory, maybe so, but in practice, the major index fund managers are fierce competitors and not likely to cooperate. (Besides, they are well aware that collusion is illegal.) Another claims that too much indexing will mess up the capital markets and their vital function in allocating capital to the most promising opportunities—but fails to provide any supporting evidence. In summary, none of the alarmist articles seems to have merit.

Finally, the benefits of indexing are increasingly being understood, and the shift from active management to indexing is accelerating. From 2012 to 2023, the share of the U.S. stock market of active mutual funds fell by 40%—from 20% to 12%—while the share of index funds more than doubled, rising from 8% to 18%. Thus, reliance on index funds has finally surpassed active mutual funds.

A major reason investors keep moving their investments into index funds is performance: For years, investors have sought out top-quartile managers. And now the data show that, over the long term, broad-based index funds achieve top-quartile results—actually, results in the top half of the top quartile.[5]

Significantly, those who have switched to indexing almost never reverse their decision and go back to tradi-

---

[5] Higher long-term returns can be obtained in "alternative" investments like private equity and venture capital. While the best of the alternative managers do achieve superior returns, the track record of success varies widely. Since most investors in these classes have to tie up their money for years (even a decade) without the opportunity to cash out, these investments are not going to be attractive unless you achieve the top-quartile returns. Those managers with the best track record of such success are in such high demand that it can be difficult for average investors to be "accepted" by such managers.

tional active investing. This is because the evidence keeps increasing and investors keep learning from their own experience that indexing is easy, costs and taxes are lower, *and* indexing achieves higher returns, particularly over the long term. And, thanks to the power of compounding, the long-term return advantages grow larger and larger.

CHAPTER FIVE

MINIMIZE YOUR COSTS, FEES, AND TAXES

I f we accept the reality that today's stock market prices are set so accurately that active investors are not going to outperform as they could and did 50 years ago, there is still a compelling opportunity to make a significant financial difference. How? By attacking in the opposite direction—not by increasing returns but by reducing costs. Most investors pay scant attention to the costs charged for investing—but you can actively reduce those costs. As Ben Franklin said, "A penny saved is a penny earned." Remember, you can only keep the money you do *not* pay out to others. Over the long term, cost control can add great value, because your investments will compound faster and lift your Power Curve higher and higher.

First in line are the fees charged by investment managers. The fees charged by active investment managers are much higher than index funds. Historically they have been as much as an annual fee of 1% of the asset value, versus a fee as low as just 0.04% for a total market index fund—25 *times* lower.

Let's take a careful look at active investment management fees. At first glance they may appear to be low; often they are described as "*only* 1%." Where did the convention of "only 1%" management fees come from? The history of fees for investment management began many decades ago when law firms in Boston, London, New York, and Philadelphia provided legal services like preparing trusts and estate plans. For these services, law firms charged hourly fees. So, when clients also wanted help with the investment aspects of trusts, lawyers naturally charged by the hour for these services too.

This concept of how to calculate fees changed substantially when a new kind of firm—an investment specialist—entered the field. Here is how one of those new firms—Scudder, Stevens & Clark—described the process of fee determination:

When in 1919, we [at Scudder, Stevens & Clark] initiated the work of Investment Counsel, we had to determine, without precedent to guide us, how to charge for our services. We did not know what it would cost us to do this work or what would be equitable for the investor to pay; we did not know whether to charge an annual fee, or a fee for each transaction executed on our advice, or whether this charge should be against principal or income. For nearly two years, therefore, we conducted our work with a view to securing data by which to solve these problems.

In regard to the basis of charge, we reached the following conclusion: that the fee for our services should be a charge against the investor's principal and not against his income from that principal. A charge based on income (the method unfortunately specified by law for trust funds) tends to emphasize income at the expense of principal, with the result that the principal may decline, involving permanent loss. If, however, principal is protected and built up, income is not only safeguarded but gradually increased and its future integrity ensured. It was apparent to us, therefore, that we should place the emphasis on principal, and that our fee should be charged against principal. We therefore reached the conclusion that the client should pay us as counsel a definite annual fee, to be determined by the amount of principal under our supervision.

The idea was new. Would investors realize the value of unbiased professional advice? For generations, [people] have fully recognized the importance of sound medical or legal advice and will pay adequately for it. A precedent had been established. We, however, had to prove that our services were worth paying for.

To demonstrate to the investor that it would be to his advantage to employ us as counsel, we would undertake, upon his request, to make a report on his affairs. If he does not like our advice, he pays us nothing. If he accepts our report in substance, he pays us 1% of the sum involved in each purchase and each sale made on our advice. We agree, however, that for a trial period of two years the total of such charges— provided this total amounts to $1,000—shall not exceed 1% of the client's principal as shown by the appraisal in our original report. By this method we establish for this period of two years a maximum charge based on a rate of ½ to 1% per year, but with no minimum. This procedure proved satisfactory both to our clients and to ourselves.[1]

For the past century, fees have been based on total *assets* invested with a manager.

---

[1] *A Professional Charge for Investment Counsel* from a Scudder, Stevens & Clark memorandum, New York, NY, January 25, 1977 (originally published 1927).

When banks offered personal trust investment services, state legislatures, noting that the assets usually were invested in pooled funds, set limits on the level of fees that could be charged. To protect widows and orphans, these fees were set at low levels, typically only 1/10th of 1%. Banks soon learned that this fee level was too low to make trust investing a profitable business and so, with a fixed ceiling on *revenues*, they concentrated on minimizing *costs*. As a result, staff compensation was low, and talented, ambitious people went elsewhere for their careers.

With fees fixed at low levels, banks found a backdoor way to increase their earnings. The trust departments of the banks would conduct their securities trading through brokerage firms at what were, half a century ago, fixed rates of commission, averaging 40 cents a share. The amount of commission business directed to specific brokerage firms was set as payment for each broker's maintaining at cooperating banks, substantial cash balances gathered from their many retail customer accounts. The banks would then lend these balances to their commercial customers and charge interest, a profitable arrangement. The rate of exchange—how much in brokerage commissions for how much in demand deposit balances—was agreed and monitored for conformance at, typically, 5–6%.

When brokerage commissions were made negotiable half a century ago, this shadow arrangement was no longer acceptable. To replace the backdoor income,[2] fees for investment services would have to be increased. Morgan Guaranty Trust Company, then the industry leader, took the lead by declaring that its trust accounts would be charged at 1/4th of 1%. This bold move had most competitors expecting Morgan Guaranty to lose substantial business. That did *not* happen. Only one small account left. All the others stayed. The larger message was clear: Low fees were not important to clients. A pattern of fee increases began and continued for the next two decades.

Context matters, particularly on pricing. "Performance" mutual funds were gaining market share in the 1960s—and gaining at increasing rates. Another new group of investment managers were rapidly gaining new institutional accounts: investment counsel firms organized specifically to

---

[2] For a few years, before fully regulated trading commissions, a few brokerage firms offered third-market transactions at low commissions. But trust departments traded with these firms *and* charged their customers the amount "saved" by using third-market firms.

serve institutional investors. These funds typically charged higher fees and "word got around" that higher fees led to superior performance. Taking the view that you get what you pay for, an increasing number of institutional investors were more than willing to pay the higher fees in hopes of getting higher returns.

Then stock brokerage firms that based their business with institutional funds on their in-depth research on major companies and industries got into the investment management business serving pension funds and endowments. Their *nominal* fees were high—high fees were increasingly accepted as an indicator of superior talent and higher expected rates of return. Since these firms were also members of the New York Stock Exchange and were required back then to charge full commissions on transactions, they would offer to offset their fees by the amount of those commissions. This, in effect, almost always meant that the *stated* fee of 1% would be *entirely* offset—so the real fee would be zero. But the nominal charge of 1% of assets was becoming established.

Increasingly, the linkage between higher fees and better investment performance became established in the minds of customers, and a multiyear upward progression of institutional investment fees continued through the 1970s and 1980s. Mutual fund fees also increased. (And the SEC supported a new kind of add-on fee under Regulation 10(b)-1 to reward retail brokers for encouraging their customers to be long-term investors and stay with their current mutual funds instead of switching to new funds.)

Active managers usually describe their fees as "only 1%," which sounds quite low; however, those fees are *not* low if viewed as a percentage of the investment return they earn for you. For example, if an active investment manager achieves a market return of 7%, while charging you "only" 1%[3] of the *assets* you have invested, that charge represents nearly 15% of your returns that year—and is actually higher once you factor in taxes and any operating costs passed onto you by the active manager. Finally, since

---

[3] For example, say you give an active manager $100,000 to invest, and the fee is "only" 1% annually—or $1,000. If that firm earns you 8%, the fee is 12.5% of what they earned for you—and higher when you factor in taxes and other costs. Plus, in the second year and every successive year, you will be charged 1% again on the entire amount you have invested with the manager—independent of how well the manager has done for you, relative to any benchmark. The same $100,000 invested in a total stock market index fund might have a fee of 0.04%—or $40.

low-cost index funds will again and again deliver almost all of the market returns, the incremental fees of most active managers are over 100% compared to the incremental returns they produce.

An important aspect of fees is that no client pays the investment manager's fee by writing out a check. Fees, as a convenience, are quietly deducted from the assets in the account. Did you ever wonder whether the acceptance of fees would be nearly as great if clients were required to write a check each year and were thus reminded of how much they were actually paying their manager?

Fees, of course, are not the only expense borne by investors. The operating costs of buying and selling securities, while small, add up. These charges are the brokerage commissions and dealer spread costs to purchase or sell stocks. These operating costs have come down in recent years but still can average 1/10th of 1% of your *assets*—and thus erode 1.5% of your 7% return.

As an individual investor, you also are likely to incur higher taxes by using an active manager rather than an index fund. Why? Because those managers have much higher turnover in their portfolios. As the stocks turn over, their sale triggers taxes if they have increased in value.

Taxes on gains for stocks sold by a manager can run annually about 1/10th to 2/10th of 1% of invested assets. (Index funds do generate capital gains from transactions in the buying and selling required for maintaining the index, but because index fund turnover is so much lower, the volume of those capital gains is also much lower than those typically generated by active managers: often 5% turnover annually versus as high as 30% by active managers.)

If you retain a Registered Investment Advisor, there is an additional charge, which may be as much as 1% of your assets—or 15% of your returns (assuming a market return of 7%).

All of these costs impact your Power Curve negatively. The real cost of active management is not just the higher fees—hard to justify as they may be each year—but in their long-term stealth impact by shifting you down to a lower Power Curve—and reducing your rate of compounding over time as the adverse impact gets bigger and bigger.

What is the real cost of this puppy? Answer: Much, much more than $25 when you factor in the costs of food, grooming, veterinary care, and the like. Similarly, in considering retaining an active investment manager, you need to determine all the costs you will incur—and appreciate

EXHIBIT 3

how, with the power of compounding, they will adversely affect your long-term investment results.

In addition to the actual expense charged to you, the real cost of active managers also includes the underperformance of most of them over time. This underperformance is a particular problem with funds that, striving to recover from poor past performance, take more risk. While that extra risk is sometimes rewarded, the SPIVA data show that poor results are all too often followed by even worse results.

Another type of cost adversity is that *clients* of active investment managers so often switch funds or managers at the wrong times or quit investing altogether after experiencing a major market decline. Other clients simply are overly cautious and conservative in the basic structure of their portfolio—most often by overinvesting in bonds (see Chapter 7).

Adding all these difficulties together, the average investor committed to active investment management can lose as much as an average of 2–3% in returns *per annum* through a combination of costs charged by active managers and advisers and extra taxes plus the self-imposed injuries by the investor (as discussed in Chapter 6). These costs can be a mighty large part of the 7% average expected rate of returns on equities *and* an even larger part of the 5% *real* returns after adjusting for inflation.[4] Over the very long term, such as three to five decades, that 2% to 3% annual slippage to a lower Power Curve can compound to evaporate a third or more of what might

---

[4] Inflation will eat up some of your returns. If there is 2% inflation and your portfolio's nominal return is 7%, your real return is 5%—*before* you factor in various costs outlined here.

have been the investor's final assets. So, to maximize your returns, you should attack in the opposite direction—and work diligently to avoid or minimize costs, fees, and taxes that managers or the government imposes on you. (See Exhibit 5.1). The long term impact is huge!

Exhibit 5.1: The Costs of Fees

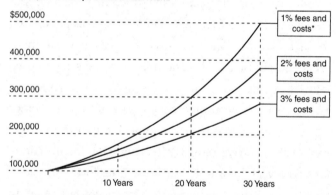

Impact of different fees and costs on an initial investment of $100,000 that reaps a 6.5% annual return.

*Costs include taxes, transaction expense, and investor errors predicted by behavioral economist (see Chapter 6).

The next chapter shows the costs that investors bring on themselves by not heeding the lessons of behavioral economics.

CHAPTER SIX

BEHAVIORAL ECONOMICS AND YOU

E ach of us is in a perpetual struggle with ourselves: We get so worried when the stock market falls that we get spooked and sell. Or we hear a stock tip from friends and want to buy (even though we should know from the last chapter and our study of markets that all the work by thousands of professional investors has already priced the stock too correctly for us to do better).

Classical economics was firmly based on the rational assumption that we act in our own best interests. That premise was put forward by Alfred Marshall[1] over 100 years ago. However, research by behavioral economists in recent decades has proven that most of us do *not* always act in our best interests—and that we are often our own worst enemies. Behavioral economists even have been able to quantify how we investors, as a group, repetitively act in ways that are *not* rational and *not* in our own interest. This reality is important for us as investors to understand—so we can protect ourselves from ourselves.

The Nobel Prize–winner Daniel Kahneman is an important teacher in this regard. His work on prospect theory with Amos Tversky deserves everyone's attention, for he showed how differently investors approach losses versus gains: Losing a dollar seems to "hurt" us twice as much as gaining a dollar pleases. This loss aversion leads us to focus on minimizing possible losses even when that means giving up potentially large gains. We are more risk

---

[1] Alfred Marshall, a British economist and author of several major books including *Principles of Economics* (1890), revolutionized how we think about supply and demand and time determining market prices.

averse than is rational and shy away from investing as much as we should in equities. We are too preoccupied by whether the stock market will go up or down next month or next year when our attention should be on the long-term record of equity returns surpassing bond returns—*and* the power of compounding.

Exhibit 6.1 shows the dramatic impact of getting spooked and stepping out of the market for even a few days. It shows what would have happened to long-term compounded returns when the few best days are removed from a record of nearly 10,000 trading days over 26 years.

Exhibit 6.1:   How Missing a Few Days in the Market Would Hurt Returns

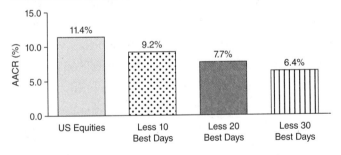

Source: Courtesy of Cambridge Associates; period covered:
January 1, 1980–April 30, 2016.

Taking out only the 10 best days—only 1/10th of 1% of the long period examined—cut the average rate of return by 19% (from 11.4% to 9.2%). Taking away the 20 next best days cut returns by an additional 17% (from 9.2% to 7.7%).

Exhibit 6.1 makes clear what can happen through our loss-adverse tendencies, and it reinforces the importance of persistence—not trying to get better results by market timing and not getting spooked by a swerve in the market.

Another major lesson from Kahneman is the illusion of control. We understandably like to feel we are in control, even when we really have little or no control. For example, investors who picked a couple of stocks that went up think they can do it again and again. Investors will enjoy greater success when, instead of looking at day-to-day changes in stock prices, they have confidence *over the long term* that a diversified portfolio of stocks (particularly in low-cost index funds) will fare better. We need to avoid thinking we have some element of control or mastery.

In his *New York Times* bestseller *Thinking, Fast and Slow* (2011), Kahneman outlines additional behavioral economics tenets that have important implications for our lives and for our investing success. We need to be aware of them so we can protect ourselves from ourselves and strive to manage our own behavior to offset our proclivity to make the same mistakes that others make. As Walt Kelly's lovable cartoon character Pogo lamented, "We have met our enemy—it is *us!*"

We are surrounded by temptations to be wrong—in investing and in life. That's why Kahneman's *Thinking, Fast and Slow* is one of the most important and valuable books successful investors can ever read. The following insights from Kahneman and other behavioral economists catalog human frailties that are important for investors to recognize, understand, and avoid.

- *Jumping to conclusions.* Acting on partial knowledge is dangerous—particularly in investing. When we buy and sell individual stocks, most of us base most of our investment decisions on remarkably limited information. All too often we allow first impressions to govern.

- *Getting distracted by extraneous information.* A classic example of misjudgment or misunderstanding is the "Linda problem" that was reviewed in *Thinking, Fast and Slow*. Linda is described as 31, single, and an outspoken philosophy student. She is deeply concerned about discrimination and social justice and participated in antinuclear demonstrations. Students were asked to rate the likelihood of several different statements. Two of these were "Linda is a bank teller" and "Linda is a bank teller and active in the feminist movement." Even though the second description is a much smaller subset of the first, 85% of group after group believed the second statement was more likely. The Linda issue arises in investing when we get distracted by extraneous information that we wrongly consider particularly relevant.

- *Preferring certainty over probabilities.* For example, if offered a choice of getting a sure $50 over a 50% chance of getting $100, most of us will go for the sure $50—even though the expected values actually are the same.

- *Reversion to the mean is powerful.* Discovered in 1886 by Francis Galton, a polymath of distinction, mean reversion is a particularly important phenomenon for understanding the behavior of market prices. An example is that very tall parents tend to have less tall children and short parents tend to have less short children. Or stocks that just went up in price are less likely to go up immediately thereafter. (There is some evidence of momentum in stock prices in the short term, but that tendency is dominated by other short-term price fluctuations.)

- *Framing effects.* The way outcomes are described can have a major impact on our views. Consider, for example, the differing impact when something is framed as half-full versus half-empty. Think carefully about how active investment managers describe their recent performance in quarterly newsletters—and focus on the actual results.

- *Availability.* We are more influenced by easy-to-see evidence, whether it is particularly valuable or not. That is why so many individuals unfortunately act on tips from TV commentators about hot stocks.

- *Avoiding faux intuition.* Intuition is divided into two categories. One is the intuition of an experienced expert in his or her field of expertise. The other is the faux intuition—the very prone-to-error judgment of an amateur with little experience.[2] The first is very likely to be right, but the second is likely to be wrong. How often do individual investors accept tips from friends and acquaintances who don't have any real expertise?

- *Fooling ourselves* by constructing fairly flimsy accounts of the past—and then believing them far more than we should.

- *Allowing the outcome to dominate our evaluation of our investment decisions,* even when the outcome involves more luck than skill.

- *Seeing anchoring effects everywhere,* particularly in decisions about money and investments. That's

---

[2] Many with little expertise in statistics, nevertheless, act on their intuition about statistical issues. How many of us would answer this question correctly? How many people are needed to have at least 50% odds of a match in the day and month (but not the year) of their birthday? Answer: 24. If 24 seems way too small, try it with a sizable group. If you can't find a large group, try it with a small group who calls out the birthdays of their parents and siblings.

why some investors say "When the stock price gets back to what I paid for it, I'll sell!" Of course, the stock market doesn't know or care about you or your intentions.

- *Seeing patterns where there are none.* A classic example is to ask a group of people to imagine they are repeatedly tossing a coin and record H (head) and T (tail) in a "random" sequence *and* also ask one person to toss a real coin and record the Hs and Ts as they occur. The actual coin-tossing record is easily identified because the truly random sequence does not *look* all that random. It will have longer runs of Hs and of Ts than we think would be random. In brief, we think random should look more "random."

Which sequence is more probable if taken from a long sequence of coin tossing?

H H H H H H H

H T H T T H T

Answer: Neither

We fall into the trap of seeing meaning where there is no meaning. So, we think we are good at seeing patterns—even when there is no pattern. Investors do this all the time: "The market was down yesterday, so it will likely be up today," or "The market was up yesterday, so chances are high that it will be up again today." No wonder we have a difficult time appreciating random walks and random numbers. We seek to find patterns, and we do "find" them, even when the data are just random.

These different kinds of anomalies in human behavior highlighted by Kahneman are important cautions in investing—and in life.

Terrance Odean and Brad Barker of the University of California Davis were the first to document the penalty to investment results from our all-too-human predilections with their 1991–1996 study of 66,000 investors' accounts. They found that the average investor underperformed the market by a stunning 6.5% during the study period when the market rose 17.9%. Later studies in lower-return markets have shown that investors repeatedly make the mistakes identified by behavioral economists that can annually cost them between 2% and 3%. More recently, DALBAR Inc., the market research firm for the financial services industry, reported that the average equity investor earned 5.5% less than the S&P return in 2023; and even over 20 years, the average shortfall per year was just over 2%.

Instead of trying to remember all the insights from behavioral economics, just remember that we investors are in a continuous struggle with our all-too-human predilections—and that we can largely avoid them by the unexciting approach of investing in low cost index funds—and just holding on.

Like Kahneman's *Thinking, Fast and Slow*, Burton Malkiel's wonderful book, *A Random Walk Down Wall Street*,[3] is replete with great insights into the behavior of investors as well as sage investment advice. Malkiel observes that "Researchers in cognitive psychology have documented that people often deviate from rationality in making judgments amid uncertainty." He goes on to point out

---

[3] Now in its 13th edition (2024).

that 80% to 90% of college students say they are more skillful and safer drivers than others in their class. These beliefs, which are clearly mathematically impossible, are common. For example, in comparison with their roommates, Malkiel tells us, students typically expect to have happier marriages, have more successful careers, and enjoy better health. And, continuing on, they expect their college roommates to have more troubles with alcoholism, divorce, and illness.

Adult men also rate themselves highly: 100% rank themselves in the top 50% and—drum roll—25% rank themselves in the top 1% in their ability to get along well with others. Moreover, 80% of us think we are "above average" in investing capability, economic and political expertise, car driving, dancing, listening to and understanding others, and our sense of humor. Obviously numerically impossible, the data convey an important message: As human beings, we give ourselves much more credit than we deserve. In investing, such overconfidence can lead to making mistakes, and those mistakes can be expensive—*very* expensive.

Both Malkiel and Kahneman lay out the many ways we humans do not act rationally. In many spheres of our lives, it is hard to avoid these pitfalls. Luckily in investing, if we choose to use low-cost index funds and follow benign neglect, we will not be continuously fussing with our investments and thus will avoid all the temptations that behavioral economics research has now proven.

The right way to view skillful investing is to see it as a long, disciplined continuous process in which the wise investor focuses on minimizing errors and improving the decision-making process. As Tommy Armour, the great golf teacher, famously said, "The key to success in golf is making fewer bad shots."[4]

Successful investing is simple—but *not* easy. It takes three strengths. First is the personal discipline to maintain a long-term focus when surrounded by many tempting and compelling distractions. Second is the ability to understand the great advantage of benign neglect—doing less—because most of the actions by most investors and most investor helpers do more harm than good. Third is the ability and discipline to think and act consistently according to your long-term plan, particularly in periods of general excitement or uncertainty. All three are important reasons to invest in index funds and exchange-traded funds.

---

[4] See his superb book, *How to Play Your Best Golf All the Time* (1995).

CHAPTER SEVEN

YOUR TOTAL FINANCIAL PORTFOLIO

Usually, when we think about our financial portfolio, we think of stocks, bonds, and cash. Our Portfolio Allocation is the percentage in each asset category. For example, someone might have 60% in stocks, 37% in bonds, and 3% in cash.

Over the long term and as has been regularly reported, stocks have outperformed bonds. A recent article states that "stocks today are poised to offer long-term patient investors a risk premium of 1–2 percent."[1] Other research has reported an even greater advantage in holding stocks. For example, Charles Schwab reported in 2019 that the difference in the prior three decades was even larger: "Over the past 30 years, stocks posted an average annual return of 10.4%, and bonds 6.8%."[2]

Even though the percentage returns in the future of owning stocks are likely to be lower than past returns—because prices today are relatively higher—the long-term returns on stock investments are virtually sure to be significantly higher than the returns on bond investments.

Since stocks outperform bonds over the long term, there has to be a good rationale for owning bonds with their lower rate of return. The usual rationale is that bonds add a more stable asset not subject to the wide, short-term fluctuations in price that often occur with stocks. Thus, bonds can offset some of the equity market's

---

[1] Toby Nangle, *Financial Times* online (December 13, 2023) quoting Rob Arnott, Research Affiliates founder.

[2] Charles Schwab, "Why Diversification Matters," online posting July 23, 2019. https://www.schwab.com/learn/story/why-diversication-matters?msockid=033 7b4664fc065b9102a7884e7e64di

volatility, but this comes at a price: 2–3% lower returns over the long term. With compounding, this lower return can have a major negative impact on an investor's eventual portfolio value.

For many decades, the conventional wisdom has been that you should "invest your age in bonds." If you were 40 years old, 40% of your portfolio would be in bonds; if you were 60, the convention was to have 60% in bonds and only 40% in equities. This conventional wisdom is flawed in two major ways. First, it ignores other factors that make each of us unique investors: our wealth, our income, our savings habits, our knowledge of investing, and our attitude toward market risk. (If someone has substantial assets, they may be less anxious about the impact of a market downturn since they feel they can weather that decline.) Second, it entirely disregards other stable assets that the typical investor has *beyond* his or her securities portfolio of stocks and bonds.

Most of us have other stable assets—"bond equivalents"—that are important parts of our Total Financial Portfolio; those assets need to be included when determining our true Portfolio Allocation. Look at *all* your major assets that have stable characteristics rather like bonds that eventually will be converted into cash and spent by you or your heirs. Include these assets in calculating the asset mix of your Total Financial Portfolio:

- **_Home._** Include it at its current market price (after deducting what's left of the mortgage) as part of the stable value, bond-like portion of your Total Financial Portfolio. The average home equity in America, according to the National Association of REALTORS®, is $407,500. Many homeowners say buying their house was "the best investment I ever made." While a family's enjoyment is a major benefit of homeownership, let's focus on just the financials. The long-term noncallable mortgage provides substantial financial leverage in making the purchase _and_ "forced saving" as the loan gets paid off. Plus, inflation gets quietly factored into the market price. Also, annual interest payments on mortgages up to $750,000[3] are tax deductible. Mortgages can

---

[3] $1 million if bought before December 16, 2017.

be viewed as an unusually positive form of debt. Yes, your home *is* your castle—emotionally—and a nice place for you and your family to live the good life. But most of the people who proudly announce "Our home has been our best investment" are comparing grapes to grapefruit and miss the point that even with these major financial advantages, most houses appreciate far less than equities over time.

- *Social Security.* Social Security will pay out benefits a lot like an enhanced annuity. Social Security is special because it's backed by the federal government—the highest possible credit—*and* every year, your benefits are increased to offset inflation. While many investors have a pretty good idea of how large their *annual* Social Security payouts will be, most of us never even think of determining the total net present value of our future Social Security benefits. Yale University Professor John Geanakoplos and Stephen Zeldes—experts in Social Security at Yale's Tobin Center—developed an analysis of benefits discounted at various real interest rates. The next table shows—for the first time—that the present value of the total Social Security payout for some of us may be larger than the value of our homes. Note that future benefits are discounted to their present value at 1%, 2%, and 3% *real* rates of return. Even at a 3% real rate, the present value of benefits is substantial, particularly for those with incomes above the 50th percentile.

Present Values by Mortality Assumption and Interest Rates of Discount

Benefit level	2022 benefit	0% real	1% real	2% real	3% real
25th percentile	$15,013	$323,052	$287,173	$257,369	$232,399
50th percentile	23,463	504,852	448,782	402,205	363,183
75th percentile	30,040	646,365	574,578	514,945	464,985
90th percentile	37,760	812,474	722,239	647,281	584,482
Maximum	50,328	1,082,897	962,629	862,721	779,020

Source: John Geanakoplos and Stephen Zeldes of Yale University's Tobin Center.

The value of Social Security benefits can be viewed as an *enhanced* bond equivalent, because payouts are increased to offset inflation.[4] Thus, they should be added to the fixed income or bond part of your Total Financial Portfolio.

- **Potential inheritance.** You may also expect an inheritance. If you do and can estimate it, include that amount too.

- **Savings from future earnings.** Your future savings from your earnings in the years to come, especially if you are not close to retirement, should be a major component of your Total Financial Portfolio. Make a conservative estimate of your ability to save in the years ahead and how these savings will likely accumulate. Decide when you will likely retire and then estimate the net present value of that future stream of savings. Your ability to earn—and save—in the future may be particularly large if you're young, have a high-paying career, and are part of a double-income couple.

---

[4] Because date of death is so uncertain, Social Security analysts might argue that benefits are comparable to equities.

You can now see that major parts of your Total Financial Portfolio are a lot like bonds: your home equity, the present value of your Social Security benefits, and your future estimated savings plus any likely inheritance. These assets should be included in your Total Financial Portfolio when deciding your asset mix—and how much you want in bonds. For example, why should *half* of a person's securities be in bonds at age 50 when that individual's Total Financial Portfolio includes large stable-value assets like their house, future Social Security benefits, and perhaps 20 more years of annual savings? "Invest your age in bonds" is *not* wise, because it ignores the reality that your Total Financial Portfolio already has substantial bond equivalents.

What *is* wise is to recognize that you can allocate a lot more of your securities portfolio to equities where you will get higher returns—compounded—over the long term.

CHAPTER EIGHT

WHEN BONDS ARE RIGHT FOR YOU

There *are* certain times—each an exception—when bonds are, indeed, advisable as part of your securities portfolio. Bonds can be splendid investments when used for the right purposes and in the right amounts. But all too often, as described in Chapter 7, bonds are owned in amounts that reflect misguided conventional wisdom and ignore the realities of particular investors.

Bonds can be the right way to invest if you know you will need the money in the near or intermediate future (say two to six years)[1] for a specific important purpose, such as college tuition or a starter home—when you don't want to be exposed to the risk of the stock market having a steep decline just when you will need the money. In such situations, you would care a lot more about price stability than the chance of a higher return. For those major spending priorities, the risks of fluctuating stock prices can and should be avoided even when the return you will get in bonds will be lower than the returns you might have gotten from investing in stocks. Fortunately, for such major commitments, you can match the time of your spending with the maturity date of bonds.

Historically, another place for bonds is for investors who want protection against having to sell stocks after a serious drop in the stock market. If you don't want to have to sell stocks to cover your expenses at a low point of the market, you may want to consider a two- to three-year "spending cushion" that you keep in bonds. If so,

---

[1] If you need access to cash in less than two years, money market securities are advisable.

dividend income from your stock portfolio will likely continue uninterrupted, and you will want a cushion just large enough to cover the cash gap between spending and dividend income and, when retired, Social Security benefits plus your 401(k) Required Minimum Distribution.

As investments, bonds have a certain positive characteristic: You know what will be paid out to you at a known time in *nominal* dollars.[2] However, you won't get more, and you might get less if the issuer defaults or if inflation diminishes the value of the dollars you'll get. To get this lower price risk, investors pay a significant near-term opportunity cost—and, far more important, the long-term cost of being on a lower Power Curve. So, remember that the opportunity cost of owning bonds over the long term can be surprisingly high.

As the review of behavioral economics showed, most of us are so focused on the disconcerting way stock market prices fluctuate over the short run that we overemphasize reducing short-term price fluctuations and underemphasize the powerful long-run *compounding* rate of returns

---

[2] But you do not know how much inflation will change the purchasing power of the dollar.

of stocks. The emphasis can and should be the other way around. When buying bonds to reduce asset fluctuations in a portfolio, carefully consider the magnitude of the opportunity cost you will be paying many years from now by such a shift to a lower and slower Power Curve. In the far future, how much will you care about today's market price changes? Will you even remember today's price fluctuations?

In Chapter 9, we turn to a far better and less costly way for investors to bring stability to their overall portfolio than bulking up on bonds: a Spending Rule adapted from the endowment model that has been developed and battle-tested by leading universities.

CHAPTER NINE

YOUR SPENDING RULE

A sensible spending rule should be a powerful part of your Save-Invest-Spend troika. All too often, spending policy is seen merely as a derivative of the current portfolio situation: "I need to liquidate some of my portfolio to cover my spending needs." We worry that our cash needs will occur when the stock market is down temporarily. To reduce this risk, we bulk up on bonds to bring stability to our securities portfolio so that our annual withdrawals will be relatively consistent over time. This is a clumsy and high-cost way to achieve a reasonably predictable stream of payouts. Instead, spending should be viewed as one of three equally important interactive components of successful long-term investing: long-term saving, long-term investing, and spending needs over the long term.

An effective Spending Rule converts the price-volatile returns of the market into far smoother, more predictable stream of payouts and enables your long-term investment strategy to focus on achieving higher long-term returns.

A sophisticated Spending Rule was developed decades ago by Yale's Nobel Laureate James Tobin for that university's endowment. Variations of the Tobin Rule have been tested by many leading universities and are increasingly used by other nonprofit institutions. Individuals can and should use a simplified version of the rule for their own investments.

Although Spending Rules vary in their details, each is a smoothing formula to ensure a relatively consistent flow of funds for spending—even as portfolio values fluctuate with the market. In designing your own spending rule, first, average the year-end values of your assets over the prior several years (preferably more than five years) to dampen the impact of market fluctuations. Next, calculate what would be a prudent withdrawal of the averaged assets—likely 4–5%—to determine what dollar amount you can prudently withdraw from your current portfolio each year to cover some of your expenses. Averaging your assets over multiple years makes the funds available for your spending far more consistent and predictable. If, for example, you settle on a 5% rate of withdrawal and a six-year moving average of the year-end value of your assets, a 30% drop in the stock market would lead to only a 5% reduction in your payout that year (and much of that reduction likely would be provided by your consistent dividend income).

Importantly, by following such a Spending Rule, you are then free to concentrate on achieving significantly higher long-term returns without the need to be overinvested in bonds. Stabilizing the investor's income with a responsible Spending Rule frees the investment portfolio to invest more in equities and produces, over time, a higher and more rapidly rising portfolio value and income stream.

Individual investors may consider gradually spending down their assets versus maintaining their value for future generations (which is the goal for most institutional endowments). If you are not particularly interested in preserving or increasing the purchasing power of your current assets in perpetuity, likely you could have a Spending Rule of 7% (or even more) for a portfolio that is all in equities—and not exhaust the corpus before you die.[1] Alternatively, if you adopt a lower Spending Rule and take out only 4% a year, the principal will likely grow over time and you will have money left after your death for family bequests or charitable gifts. Whatever path is chosen, the individual who understands his or her Power Curve of compounding and takes advantage of the long, long term when making investment policy decisions will enjoy a new kind of financial freedom by adopting a personal Spending Rule[2] instead of having a portfolio unduly laden with low-return bonds.

---

[1] Another benefit of working longer is that there are fewer years in retirement that would need to be covered from savings.

[2] If the rate of spending by an individual or institution is beyond the portfolio's ability to support it, the simple, but surely not easy, first response would be to consider ways of reducing the level of spending.

CHAPTER TEN

DEFERRING SOCIAL SECURITY BENEFITS AND WORKING LONGER

Two of our most important investment decisions are ones most of us get most wrong: (1) when we should begin Social Security payments and (2) when we should stop working. Sadly, most of us don't even know how important these decisions can be, because we don't appreciate the magnitude of the impact they can have on the last decades of our lives.

We all know that we can decide—within limits—when to start collecting our Social Security benefits, and most of us know the earliest age at which we can claim the monthly benefit is age 62. Nearly as many of us know we must claim Social Security benefits by age 70½. But only a few of us know how much more we will get—year after year—if we wait to start receiving Social Security benefits until we are 70½.[1]

Ask financial people how much more in benefits a worker will get by waiting those 8½ years from 62 to 70½ to start Social Security payouts and you'll usually get answers like this: "I don't know the exact amount of the increase, but it must be a lot. At least 20% and maybe even 30%!" An impressive difference? Yes. But it's wrong—way wrong! *It's way too small!*

The actual increase in annual benefits is 8% each year. Over 8½ years, that compounds to—drum roll—76%!

---

[1] The Social Security Administration adds to our confusion by defining full retirement age as 65.

Plus, those larger benefits continue for as long as you live *and* will be increased each year to offset inflation. So, it's important to think carefully about when you will elect to begin taking Social Security benefits. Remember that retiring and claiming your Social Security benefits are separate decisions: You can stop working *before* you reach 70½ *and* still collect much larger Social Security monthly benefit checks *if* you wait and start receiving your benefits when you are 70½.[2]

That's not all. If you decide to keep working, there are important additional benefits. For most of us, our expenses tend to decline in our 60s because the home mortgage has been paid off and the children are on their own. So, our 60s are a particularly good time for us to save more. By continuing to work after age 62 and not taking money *out* of the 401(k) plan each year *and* putting more money *into* the plan each of those additional 8½ years, you can more than double your 401(k) plan assets—and your annual payouts.

---

[2] Of course, for those with serious medical conditions, claiming benefits early may be prudent since you may expect not to live as long as the average citizen.

Finally, if you work longer and defer your Social Security payouts, you can combine the 76% increase in Social Security benefits with the increased payout from your much larger 401(k) fund, and your annual income during retirement increases handsomely. That's why for many working Americans, deciding when to claim Social Security and deciding whether to work longer are two of our most important investment decisions. Tell your friends!

CHAPTER ELEVEN

YOUR PERSONAL INVESTMENT PLAN

You are now ready to create your Personal Investment Plan. It will consist of three parts: your Portfolio Allocation, your Savings Plan, and your Spending Rule.

Your Portfolio Allocation is the percentage targets of equities versus bonds versus cash that you determine you should hold. Make sure you do not automatically apply some outdated rule of thumb about investing your age in bonds. In order to get your Portfolio Allocation correct, you will need to:

- Specify your financial objectives, outlining your minimum annual needs—and also your hope-to-have aspirations.
- Make reasonable estimates of your future earning power and savings.
- Inventory the assets in your Total Financial Portfolio, including estimates of the value of all your bond-like assets.

After that assessment, you will be ready to determine what asset allocation is right for you. You now know that you need to factor in all parts of your Total Financial Portfolio—including your home, Social Security benefits, and others—so you don't allocate too much to bonds. Additionally, you know you can benefit from the magic of compounding and the higher return of investing in equity index funds with their lower fees, costs, and taxes—and their protection from the perils of behavioral economics.

While all investors care about the current earnings and dividends of the companies they invest in, long-term investors care much more about the prospects for companies' future earnings and future dividends because they are powerful determinants of value. The dividend yield on *today's* price in future years—10, 20, even 40 from now—is impressive. This is not surprising—unless we forget the power of compounding. As long-term investors, our principal focus should always be on the power of compounding and how it can serve our purposes wonderfully for the long run if we start early enough.

We know that in the long run, stocks produce higher returns than bonds. However, we also know that in the short or medium run, stock prices fluctuate more—much more. So each of us must consider the eventual benefits of owning a portfolio of stocks over the long term. One way to achieve that understanding is to study investment and market history and strive to internalize the major lessons. To make the point, consider how much price difference there is in a single stock on a single day annualized. If a $40 stock has a pricing range from the day's high to the same day's low of $1, that price range, multiplied by 250 trading days, would amount to an incredible $250 "variation." Even over a month, that theoretical price range would be absurd. This thought experiment raises an important question: Why should a long-term investor care at all about the day-to-day or month-to-month fluctuations in stock prices if he or she is not planning to sell any time soon? Because, since we are all human, we pay far too much attention to short-term price fluctuations than we should, and this can distract us from the long-term run rate, or trend.

Remember that the statement "less is more" by the great architect Mies van der Rohe applies to most investors. If we are less active and make fewer decisions, we will make fewer mistakes. That's why most investors will enjoy better long-term results if they limit themselves to just 20 major investing decisions—about one every three years—over their lifetimes. The results will be even better if those decisions are made only because of significant changes—*not* in the securities market but in the particular circumstances of the investor. The benefits of benign neglect can be formidable. There is strong evidence that many investors make costly mistakes in each of the following categories:

- *Market timing*—particularly large-scale decisions to get out of the market, usually made *after* a major decline
- *Changing portfolio structure*—particularly when made in response to recent market changes
- *Changing managers*—both terminating and hiring can incur slippage costs

* * * *

I hope this very short book has given you the confidence to develop a very long-term investment plan—and to have the discipline to stay with it through the ups and downs of the market. However, if you think you need some professional advice, you might investigate the services of a Registered Investment Advisor (RIA). RIAs are registered with the Securities and Exchange Commission or a state equivalent and, unlike broker-dealers, have a fiduciary duty to put the best interests of their clients first. (Of course, like any professional, there are better or worse practitioners, and you should do your homework before retaining one.)

Usually these investment advisors prefer to work with you on an ongoing basis, charging a fee, based on a percentage of your securities portfolio. You might be wise to explore retaining an RIA at a very handsome hourly rate to help you create your long-term Personal Investment Plan that you should not need to alter often. This arrangement will prove far less expensive than a recurring annual fee and will provide you with what you really need.

The most important positive step any investor can take—and all investors should take—is figuring out what your objectives as an investor are—offensive and defensive—and then designing your long-term plan in ways that maximize your pro and minimizes your con. Developing the discipline to stay consistently on your plan allows the inevitable positives of your Power Curve to work their magic for you.[1]

---

[1] Educating yourself by reading the following books on investing will reinforce your staying on course: Burton Malkiel's *A Random Walk Down Wall Street* (50th anniversary edition, 2024); Benjamin Graham's *The Intelligent Investor*, with new commentary by Jason Zweig (2024); or my *Winning the Loser's Game* (8th ed., 2021).

SUMMARY

Successful investing *is* simple—but *not* easy. It takes several strengths. First is the personal discipline to save. Next is developing a long-term investment program and maintaining a long-term focus when surrounded by the many tempting distractions of the present. Third is the self-discipline of benign neglect—doing less—because most of the actions by most investors and most investor helpers do more harm than good. The final strength is the ability and discipline to think and act consistently according to your long-term investment plan, particularly in periods of general excitement or uncertainty. Throughout, you need to have the courage to be patient and let time and compounding work for you. All of these are important reasons to invest in index funds and exchange-traded funds (ETFs).

Today, every investor has three great gifts of extraordinary importance that have been explored in this short book. The first two great gifts are *time* and *compounding*. The third great gift—low-cost index funds and ETFs—could only have come into existence after the securities markets had changed enough to make it highly unlikely that active managers—after fees, taxes, and operating costs—would be able, over the long run, to beat the market or even keep up. That's why low-cost index funds so consistently rank in the top quartile of all mutual funds in long-term performance. As we have seen, index investors are less active and far less likely to get provoked into the changes that behavioral economists keep showing are so costly to investors' long-term results. Benign neglect in investment operations is the rewarding friend of investors who are comfortable in index funds.

To succeed as a long-term investor:

- Save as much as you can as early as you comfortably can.
- Minimize costs that lower your Power Curve rate of return.

- Invest in index funds and ETFs that save you money in low fees, low taxes, and low operating costs—and as importantly, protect you from the major costs identified by behavioral economists.
- Emphasize equities in the securities part of your Total Financial Portfolio.
- Use a smoothing Spending Rule to generate predictable payouts and avoid overreliance on bonds.
- Defer claiming Social Security.
- Keep your focus on your long-term goals and investment program.

Then you will have the long-term success you seek. Bon voyage!

ACKNOWLEDGMENTS

E very book has its own origin story, and this short book has a long one when you include my many decades of consulting with and learning from the world's leading investment managers.

This book really began when my friend Anne asked how a long-term investor should think about long-term investing. When friends Philippe and Nan-b posed the same central question, I realized it was an important one for everyone who wants to take investing as a serious long-term responsibility.

Candidly, most investors and most investment advisors are overly focused on the market's short-term behavior and give far too little attention to the important reality that they and their families will be investing for more than 50 years.

Also, many investors do not seem to appreciate the importance of the major changes in the markets over the past 50 years and their impact on what does and does not work for investors.

The time has come for all investors to rethink the major concepts of investment management. My hope is that this short book has served as a useful guide.

Burt Malkiel, my colleague and friend over several decades, not only wrote the introduction but also made important contributions to the text. My son Chad created several helpful graphics and provided superb editorial advice. My friends Brett Barakett, Carla Knobloch, James Choi, Jenny Harrington, and Paul Horne made stellar suggestions that improved the presentation and the illustrations. And I am indebted to Kelly Lorimer for innumerable rescues of the text and technology. Linda Lorimer, the love of my life, encouraged me to persist, challenged my thinking, and on every level—macro, mezzo, and micro—provided skillful editorial insights and suggestions that clarified every aspect of the text.

—**Charles D. Ellis**
New Haven, Connecticut